AF413924

4

PEACE, LAND, AND
NOTES

Iskra Books
US | UK | Ireland
www.iskrabooks.org

Iskra Books is an independent scholarly publisher—publishing original works of revolutionary theory, history, education, and art, as well as edited collections, new translations, and critical republications of older works.

ISBN-13: 979-8-8690-7127-9 (*Softcover*)

British Library Cataloguing in Publication Data
A catalogue record for this book is available from the British Library

Library of Congress Cataloging-in-Publication Data
A catalog record for this book is available from the Library of Congress

Cover Design, Typesetting, and Art by Ben Stahnke

4

PEACE, LAND, AND **NOTES**

A Study Journal and Notebook for Organizers, Students, and Educators

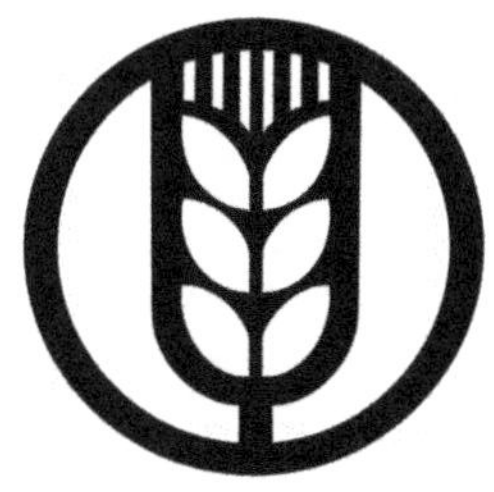

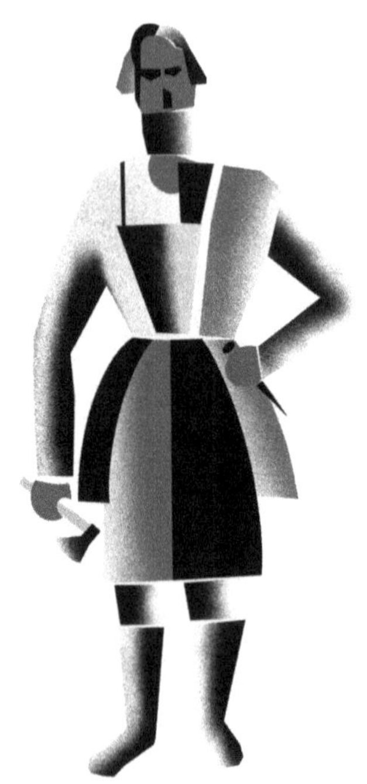

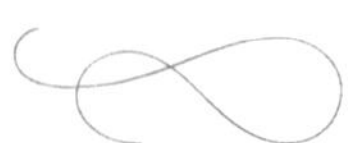

"We must have faith in the masses and we must have faith in the Party. These are two cardinal principles. If we doubt these principles, we shall accomplish nothing."

Mao Zedong

CORE TOPICS

PAGE #

"[N]o revolutionary movement is complete without
its poetical expression."

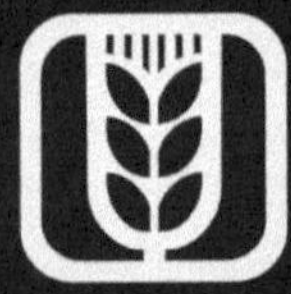

SECTION TOPICS

PAGE#

FOOTNOTES:

Theme: ____

FOOTNOTES:

Theme: ____

FOOTNOTES:

Footnotes:

FOOTNOTES:

FOOTNOTES:

FOOTNOTES:

FOOTNOTES:

"Communism is the riddle of history solved, and it knows itself to be this solution."

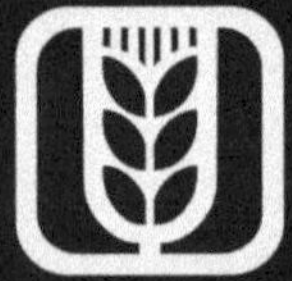

SECTION TOPICS

PAGE#

FOOTNOTES:

FOOTNOTES:

Footnotes:

FOOTNOTES:

FOOTNOTES:

FOOTNOTES:

FOOTNOTES:

FOOTNOTES:

FOOTNOTES:

"[W]ar destroys the appearance which leads us
to believe in peaceful social evolution; in the
omnipotence and the untouchability of bourgeois
legality; in national exclusivism; in the stability
of political conditions; in the conscious direction
of politics by these 'statesmen' or parties; in the
significance capable of shaking up the world
of the squabbles in bourgeois parliaments; in
parliamentarism as the so-called center of social
existence."

ROSA LUXEMBURG
1904

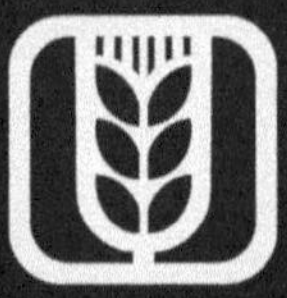

SECTION TOPICS

PAGE #

FOOTNOTES:

FOOTNOTES:

FOOTNOTES:

FOOTNOTES:

FOOTNOTES:

FOOTNOTES:

FOOTNOTES:

FOOTNOTES:

Footnotes:

"They who look with indifference on life all round them 'from the writer's carriage window' will never become a real writer [...]. There is often a great deal of snobbish conceit in budding writers—and even frequently in workers' children, but [it] has to be thoroughly washed away."

Nadezhda Krupskaya
1936

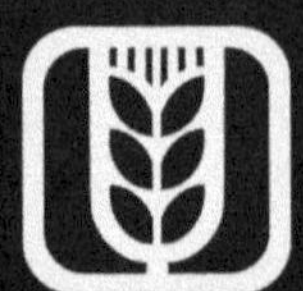

SECTION TOPICS

PAGE #

FOOTNOTES:

Footnotes:

FOOTNOTES:

Footnotes:

Footnotes:

FOOTNOTES:

FOOTNOTES:

FOOTNOTES:

FOOTNOTES:

"Colonization, in order to enjoy a certain security,
always needs to create and maintain a psychological
climate favourable to its justification: hence the
negation of the cultural, moral and intellectual values
of the subjected people; that is why the struggle
for national liberation is only complete when, once
disengaged from the colonial apparatus, the country
becomes conscious of the negative values deliberately
injected into its life, thought and traditions."

AHMED SÉKOU TOURÉ
1959

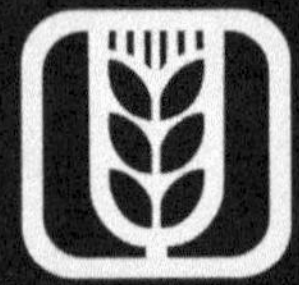

SECTION TOPICS

PAGE #

FOOTNOTES:

FOOTNOTES:

FOOTNOTES:

FOOTNOTES:

FOOTNOTES:

FOOTNOTES:

FOOTNOTES:

Footnotes:

Footnotes:

"The strength of an organization lies in the precise coordination of its parts, in strict correspondence of various mutually connected functions. This coordination is maintained through constant growth in tektological variety, but not without bounds: [...] there comes a moment when the parts of the whole become too differentiated in their organization and their resistance to the surrounding environment weakens. This leads sooner or later to disorganization."

ALEXANDER BOGDANOV
1922

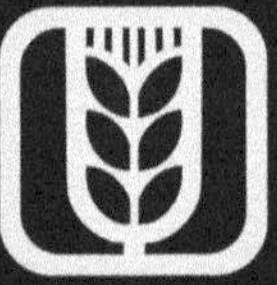

SECTION TOPICS

PAGE#

FOOTNOTES:

FOOTNOTES:

FOOTNOTES:

FOOTNOTES:

FOOTNOTES:

Footnotes:

FOOTNOTES:

FOOTNOTES:

Footnotes:

"The defeats, the failures of the European proletariat
have their origin in the mediocre positivism
with which timid union bureaucrats and bland
parliamentary teams cultivate a [...] lazy spirit in the
masses. A proletariat without more of an ideal than
a reduction of the work hours and a salary raise of
the few cents will never be capable of agrand historic
entreprise."

JOSÉ CARLOS MARIÁTEGUI
1927

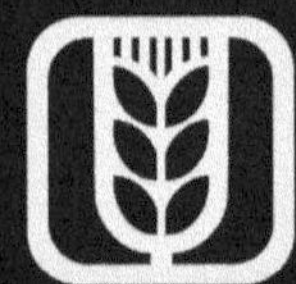

SECTION TOPICS

PAGE #

FOOTNOTES:

FOOTNOTES:

FOOTNOTES:

FOOTNOTES:

Footnotes:

PEACE, LAND, AND NOTES

FOOTNOTES:

FOOTNOTES:

Footnotes:

Footnotes:

"We are in total opposition to America's white racism,
to poverty, hunger, the systematic destruction of our
patrimony; we oppose the rich getting richer, the poor
getting poorer, and are in total opposition to wars of
aggression and imperialism, whoever pursues them."

HARRY HAY
1969

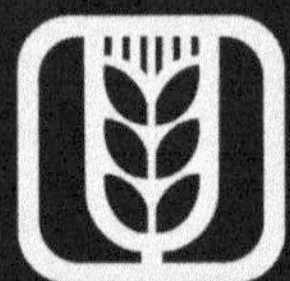

SECTION TOPICS

PAGE#

FOOTNOTES:

Footnotes:

Footnotes:

FOOTNOTES:

FOOTNOTES:

FOOTNOTES:

Footnotes:

FOOTNOTES:

FOOTNOTES:

Footnotes:

Footnotes:

www.ingramcontent.com/pod-product-compliance
Lightning Source LLC
Chambersburg PA
CBHW041559160726
48006CB00042B/2306